WITHDRAWN

W9-BHY-426

WITHDRAWN

Valentine's Day

LET'S see

by Natalie M. Rosinsky

Content Adviser: Dr. Alexa Sandmann, Professor of Literacy,
The University of Toledo; Member, National Council for the Social Studies

Reading Adviser: Dr. Linda D. Labbo, Department of Reading Education,
College of Education, The University of Georgia

Let's See Library
Compass Point Books
Minneapolis, Minnesota

Compass Point Books
3722 West 50th Street, #115
Minneapolis, MN 55410

Visit Compass Point Books on the Internet at *www.compasspointbooks.com* or e-mail your
request to *custserv@compasspointbooks.com*

Cover: Valentine's Day box of candy

Photographs ©: Laurette Alexander, cover; Lyn Hughes/Corbis, 4, 12, 18; Bettmann/Corbis, 6;
North Wind Picture Archives, 8; Reuters NewMedia Inc./Corbis, 10; Adam Woolfitt/Corbis, 14;
Museum of the City of New York/Corbis, 16; Paul A. Souders/Corbis, 20; John Cross/The Free Press, 24.

Editor: Catherine Neitge
Photo Researcher: Svetlana Zhurkina
Photo Selector: Catherine Neitge
Designer: Melissa Voda

Library of Congress Cataloging-in-Publication Data
Rosinsky, Natalie M. (Natalie Myra)
    Valentine's Day / by Natalie M. Rosinsky; reading adviser, Linda D. Labbo.
        v. cm.— (Let's see library)
    Includes bibliographical references and index.
    Contents: What is Valentine's Day?—How did Valentine's Day begin?—Who was Saint Valentine?—What
did people believe about Valentine's Day?—How has Valentine's Day changed?—What are some signs of
Valentine's Day?—What is the story of Valentine cards?—How is Valentine's Day observed in the United States?—
How is Valentine's Day observed around the world?
        ISBN 0-7565-0393-0 (hardcover)
    1. Valentine's Day—Juvenile literature. [1. Valentine's Day. 2. Holidays.] I. Title. II. Series.
    GT4925 .R67 2002
    394.2618—dc21
                                                                        2002003044

© 2003 by Compass Point Books
All rights reserved. No part of this book may be reproduced without written permission from the publisher. The publisher takes no
responsibility for the use of any of the materials or methods described in this book, nor for the products thereof.
Printed in the United States of America.

Table of Contents

What Is Valentine's Day?

On February 14, we think about people we love. We also think about friends. We may send these special people messages called **valentines**. It is fun to make or choose these decorated greetings. It feels good to get them! We sometimes give and get gifts. February 14 is Valentine's Day.

Valentine's Day is not a national holiday. Schools, government offices, and businesses are open on February 14. Still, Valentine's Day has been observed as a special day for a long time.

▲ *An umbrella shields a Valentine's Day box of candy from the snow.*

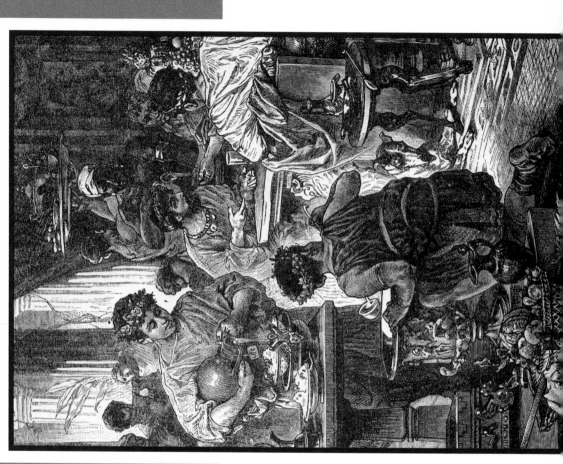

How Did Valentine's Day Begin?

Before **Christianity**, people in **Rome** sang, danced, and feasted on February 15. Their calendar put February in springtime. They welcomed the returning birds. They thought about starting families themselves. The names of young women were put in a bowl. When a man picked out a name, he was supposed to have found his love!

Later, Christian church leaders tied these **customs** to stories about Valentine. He was a priest in the city of Rome. He lived in the third century. He was named a saint after his death.

▲ *Ancient Romans celebrated in the spring.*

7

Who Was Saint Valentine?

One story says that Valentine helped young people in love. Soldiers were not allowed to marry. As a priest, Valentine broke this law. He secretly married couples who came to him.

Another story says that Valentine refused to give up Christianity. He was put in prison. A guard there had a blind daughter. Gentle Valentine became her friend. He wrote her a letter, signed "from your Valentine." When the girl held this letter, she was suddenly able to see!

Rome's ruler had Valentine killed on February 14. It became his special day.

▲ *Valentine was a priest who helped young people in love.*

What Did People Believe About Valentine's Day?

Love remained important on Valentine's Day. In France and Italy, feasts were held. Young men and women paired off. However, these couples did not always find true love together. After many years, the governments stopped these feasts.

There were foolish ideas about the day, too. In England, women thought they would marry the man they dreamed about on Valentine's Day. In Italy, women believed they would marry the first man they saw on Valentine's Day.

Love is still important today, though. Many couples get engaged or married on February 14.

▲ *Brides and grooms enter Universal Studios in Los Angeles on a recent Valentine's Day. They were among 1,000 couples married there that day.*

How Has Valentine's Day Changed?

People no longer believe that Valentine's Day brings true love. Many people, though, not just Christians, use this day to send messages of love. Valentine's Day was once just about **romantic love**. Today, valentines are sent to family and friends, too. Valentines are usually gentle and sweet, but some have jokes.

Before most people could read, valentines were spoken or sung. Today, they are usually written. All valentines were once handmade. Today, many cards are manufactured. Valentine shapes and decorations continue to suggest love.

▲ *A dog waits outside a New York post office right before Valentine's Day. Many valentines are mailed every February.*

What Are Some Symbols of Valentine's Day?

The heart is the main **symbol** of Valentine's Day. It is said to be the center of feelings. Many valentines are heart-shaped. Because real hearts are red or pink, these colors are important on Valentine's Day.

Flowers that first appear in spring are popular on valentines. Birds and butterflies that return each spring also decorate valentines.

Some valentines show a young boy with wings. He is holding a bow and arrow. This is **Cupid**, an ancient god of Rome. People believed that some- one hit by Cupid's arrow would fall in love.

▲ *Cupid decorates a garden fountain.*

What Is the Story of Valentine Cards?

In the past, people gave handmade valentines in person. Often, these paper valentines were cut or folded in fancy ways. In the nineteenth century, it became cheaper to mail letters. People wanted to send more cards. Companies began to manufacture valentines. Most of these companies were in England and the United States.

Valentine cards had many decorations. **Lace,** ribbons, and feathers were added. Some cards had pockets that hid treats. Some valentines even had parts that moved. Famous artists sometimes created the pictures for valentines.

▲ *This fancy cutout valentine was handmade about 1790.*

How Is It Observed in the United States?

Romantic valentines are popular. Family and friends give each other valentines, too. In schools, children also observe Valentine's Day. There are parties, games, and cards. One custom is the valentine box. Each student gets a card from everyone else in class. These valentines sometimes show cartoon or movie characters.

Red hearts or Cupids decorate rooms. People enjoy heart-shaped cakes, cookies, and candy. Giving chocolates in a heart-shaped box is one custom. Sometimes people give flowers or jewelry. Dances are another custom on Valentine's Day.

▲ *Heart-shaped cakes are ready for Valentine's Day.*

How Is It Observed Around the World?

Valentine's Day is a special time in other countries, too. In England, mailboxes are stuffed with cards on this day. Children as well as adults get valentines and sweet treats.

Some valentine customs differ. For example, red roses are most popular in the United States, Germany, and Mexico. In Denmark, though, white flowers called snowdrops are the valentine favorite.

The United States and England are the countries with the most Valentine's Day customs.

▲ *Valentine's Day is celebrated around the world. In the Philippines, young band members march in a Valentine's Day parade.*

Glossary

Christianity—the faith that believes Jesus Christ is the son of God

Cupid—ancient Roman god of romantic love; also, the son of Venus, goddess of love

custom—something regularly done by a group of people

lace—cloth with many patterns made by narrow threads

romantic love—love that can lead to marriage or to two people choosing to spend their lives together

symbol—something that represents something else

Rome—a city that long ago ruled many lands

valentines—written and decorated messages of love

Did You Know?

• There may have been two priests named Valentine. This is why there are different stories about this saint.

• The oldest paper valentine ever found was written about 1415. It is kept in the British Museum in London.

• Some sailors used knives to carve their valentines on whale bones.

Want to Know More?

In the Library

Bulla, Clyde Robert. *The Story of Valentine's Day*. New York: HarperCollins, 1999.

Fradin, Dennis Brindell. *Valentine's Day*. Hillside, NJ: Enslow, 1990.

Lovelace, Maud Hart. *The Valentine Box*. New York, Thomas Y. Crowell, 1966.

On the Web

Valentine Exhibition

http://www.americanantiquarian.org/Exhibitions/Valentines/

To view an exhibit of old American valentines and learn their history

Valentine's Fun for Kids

http://www.kidsturncentral.com/holidays/valentines.htm

To find Valentine's Day word searches, jigsaw puzzles, trivia, and crafts

Through the Mail

National Valentine Collectors Association

P.O. Box 1401

Santa Ana, CA 92702

For information about meetings or displays of valentines in your state

On the Road

Lincoln-Douglas Valentine Museum

101 North Fourth Street

Quincy, Illinois 62301-2900

217/224-3355 or 217/224-5767

To see old and unusual valentine cards and special, heart-shaped candy boxes

Hallmark Visitors Center

Kansas City Crown Center

Kansas City, MO 64141

816/274-3613

To learn about the famous greeting card maker and enjoy family activities

Index

About the Author

Natalie M. Rosinsky writes about history, science, and other fun things. One of her two cats usually sits on her computer as she works in Mankato, Minnesota. Both cats pay close attention as she and her family make and eat special holiday foods. Natalie earned graduate degrees from the University of Wisconsin and has been a high school and college teacher.